The Story of Google, the Search Engine that Changed the World

Emily Roberts

Copyright © 2023 by Emily Roberts.

The story of Google, the search engine that changed the world

All rights reserved. No part of this publication may be reproduced, distributed, or transmitted in any form or by any means, including photocopying, recording, or other electronic or mechanical methods, without the prior written permission of the author, except in the case of brief quotations embodied in critical reviews and certain other non-commercial uses permitted by copyright law.

Chapter 1: The Birth of a Vision 1

- Introduce the founders Larry Page and Sergey
Brin and their early lives and education.
- Explore the initial concept of PageRank
and the creation of the Google search engine.
- Highlight the early challenges and successes.

Chapter 2: Garage to Googleplex 10

- Discuss Google's early days in a garage
and its rapid growth.
- Explore the company's first office spaces,
employees, and culture.
- Describe the evolution of the Google brand.

Chapter 3: The Google Algorithm 16

- Dive into the technical aspects of
Google's search algorithm.
- Explain the significance of PageRank
and how it revolutionized search.
- Discuss the ongoing efforts to refine the algorithm.

Chapter 4: Competition and Collaboration 24

- Explore Google's early competitors and
how it outpaced them.

- Discuss key partnerships, like the Yahoo
and AOL deals, and their impact.
- Examine the evolving landscape of search engines.

Chapter 5: The Dot-Com Bubble 32

- Describe Google's experience during
the dot-com bubble.
- Explain how the company managed to
survive and thrive in a turbulent market.
- Highlight the decision to go public and its implications.

Chapter 6: Beyond Search: Google's Expanding 39
Universe

- Discuss Google's expansion beyond
search into products like Gmail, Maps, and YouTube.
- Explore the company's acquisitions and investments.
- Analyze the diversification of Google's portfolio.

Chapter 7: Google in the Spotlight 48

- Address the growing influence and public
scrutiny of Google.
- Explore issues related to privacy, antitrust,
and data collection.
- Discuss Google's responses to these challenges.

Chapter 8: Alphabet Inc.: A New Chapter   57

- Introduce the formation of Alphabet Inc.
and the restructuring of Google.
- Discuss the rationale behind this
transformation and its implications.
- Explore the various subsidiary companies
under Alphabet.

Chapter 9: The Innovations of Tomorrow   65

- Examine Google's ventures into emerging
technologies like self-driving cars and
artificial intelligence.
- Highlight projects like DeepMind and Waymo
and their potential impact on the future.
- Discuss Google's commitment to innovation.

Chapter 10: Google's Global Impact   73

- Explore the global reach of Google's
products and services.
- Discuss the company's role in shaping the
internet and information access worldwide.
- Reflect on Google's legacy and its ongoing
influence on society.

Chapter 1

The Birth of a Vision

1.1 The vision and invention of Google's co-founders, Larry Page and Sergey Brin, have had a significant impact on how people find and use information online. Their early life and education played a key influence in defining their journey towards developing one of the world's most powerful and famous technological firms.

On March 26, 1973, in Lansing, Michigan, Larry Page entered this world. His mother, Gloria Page, also taught computer programming, while his father, Carl Victor Page, taught computer science at Michigan State University. The early influence of academia and technology on Larry's childhood cannot be overstated. He had a reputation for curiosity and showed early promise in the fields of math and computer technology.

In contrast, Sergey Brin entered the world on the 21st of August, 1973, in Moscow, Russia. When he was six years old, his family fled the anti-Semitism that was sweeping the Soviet Union for a new life in the United States. Sergey Brin was raised with a strong work ethic and a love of learning by his parents, Michael and Eugenia. Sergey's upbringing instilled in him a respect for learning and a dedication to discovery.

In the mid-1990s, Larry Page and Sergey Brin met each other for the first time at Stanford University, when they were both working on their Ph.D.s. Larry was investigating the mathematical features of the web's connection structure as part of his dissertation research. Sergey, a year ahead of his classmates, enrolled in Stanford's Computer Science program and was placed on a team with Larry. They connected via their enthusiasm for the internet's limitless possibilities, which brought them closer together.

It was during their time at Stanford that Larry and Sergey launched on the journey that would ultimately lead to the founding of Google. They came up with a revolutionary idea they called PageRank to improve the ranking and organization of websites in SERPs. It was a radical break from the previous keyword-based search engines that PageRank gave web pages significance depending on the amount and quality of links referring to them.

Larry Page and Sergey Brin's chemistry was palpable from the start. Larry's mathematical expertise and Sergey's technical savvy made for a formidable duo, and they complimented one other beautifully. They shared a vision of establishing a search engine that supplied consumers with highly relevant and reliable search results, which would ultimately lead to the birth of Google.

Importantly, Larry and Sergey incorporated Google as a privately held firm in 1998. One of the founders of Sun Microsystems, Andy Bechtolsheim, invested heavily in the company at the outset. Because of the massive amount of data that can be indexed by the service, the name "Google" was taken from the mathematical phrase "googol," which is the number 1 followed by 100 zeros.

Their meteoric rise from a humble beginning as a search engine was fueled by an unwavering dedication to improving the customer experience. The two young men who met at Stanford University and set out on a journey that would forever change the way we access information were driven by passion, intellect, and shared vision. Today, Google is synonymous with internet search and offers a wide range of products and services. Inspiring ambitious entrepreneurs and inventors around the world, Larry Page and Sergey Brin's early life and education laid the groundwork for their incredible success.

1.2 The introduction of PageRank and the birth of the Google search engine were a watershed milestone in the development of the internet, ushering in a new era in the accessibility and organization of data on the web. This idea, conceived by Larry Page and Sergey Brin while they were students at Stanford University, became the basis for what is now one of the most influential technology corporations in the world.

While Larry Page and Sergey Brin were attending Stanford University to earn their Ph.D.s in the mid-1990s, the internet was rapidly growing and a plethora of new resources were being made available. Keyword-based algorithms were the mainstay of the time's preexisting search engines in their quest to return results most relevant to users' queries. However, the conclusions that these algorithms provided were either contradictory or irrelevant.

Google was created by Larry Page and Sergey Brin when they realized the shortcomings of keyword-based algorithms and set out to create a more effective, efficient, and universal system for ranking online pages. Their breakthrough was to focus on the structure of the web itself, specifically the way web sites were interconnected by hyperlinks. They theorized that a page's significance and relevance might be gauged by the number and quality of inbound links.

In honor of Larry Page, they dubbed the idea they developed PageRank, and it became the backbone of their new search engine. PageRank calculated a score for every website based on the quantity and quality of backlinks leading there. Simply said, a higher PageRank means that a website has more and better quality links connecting to it, increasing the likelihood that it will be displayed at the top of search results.

What made PageRank innovative was its ability to address the issue of relevance more effectively than keyword-based algorithms. It considered the "votes" that individual web pages received from the hyperlinks that led to them. By allowing websites to "vote" for one other's significance through connections, it "democratized" the web. Since pages with greater PageRank scores were considered more authoritative and relevant to user searches, this method significantly enhanced the quality of search results.

To bring their notion to life, Larry and Sergey began working on their own search engine, which they initially called "Backrub." This prototype was created with the intention of spidering the web, indexing web pages, and assigning PageRank values to each page. The term "Backrub" was chosen because its creators believed that the search engine would rank results based on the quality of the links leading to them.

Backrub eventually became the Google search engine, but Larry and Sergey's dedication to improving the user experience never wavered. Their goal was to provide users with quick, accurate access to information. They tweaked their algorithms and added more web sites to their index.

Larry and Sergey founded Google in 1998, and that same year, they received their first large investment and became a publicly traded corporation. The company chose to take its name from the mathematics word "googol" to convey the enormity of data that could be indexed by their search engine.

The introduction of Google changed the way that people looked for information online. By raising the bar for precision and relevance, Google's search algorithm and PageRank revolutionized the search industry. The ingenuity of Google's founders and the introduction of PageRank have permanently altered the way we interact with the internet. It's a monument to the power of inventive thinking and a commitment to improve user experiences.

1.3 The voyage of Google, the search engine that revolutionized the world, was not without its early obstacles and accomplishments. While working to deliver their innovative search engine to the masses, Larry Page and Sergey Brin encountered significant challenges. Despite these setbacks, the pair also achieved astounding successes that paved the way for Google's spectacular climb.

Initial Difficulties:

The Limitations of Current Technology The insufficient technological infrastructure of the late 1990s was a major obstacle. When the internet was still in its infancy, the enormous technical challenge of indexing its ever-growing content was daunting. In order to effectively crawl, index, and rank online sites, Page and Brin were forced to go outside the box.

Money, number two. In its infancy, Google ran into financial difficulties similar to those of many other firms. At the outset, Larry Page and Sergey Brin used their own cash and borrowed hardware resources from Stanford University to fund their endeavor. When Andy Bechtolsheim initially invested heavily in the company in 1998, they finally had the financial backing they needed to keep going.

Thirdly, [Competition:] The search engine market was already congested with established companies like Yahoo, AltaVista, and Excite. Google needed to set themselves out from the competition and get people to start using their search engine instead of the competition's.

Fourth, Scaling: The demand for servers increased as the number of people using Google rose. It was a major problem to scale their infrastructure to accommodate the rising number of website pages and user queries. They had to keep putting money into things like data centers, servers, and networks.

Early Achievements:

PageRank Algorithm 1. The invention of the PageRank algorithm was a remarkable success. By prioritizing the quality and amount of links connecting to online pages, it delivered more accurate and relevant search results. With this breakthrough, Google was able to differentiate itself from its rivals and build the framework for its groundbreaking search engine.

Second, a Minimalist Approach: When compared to the crowded and ad-heavy interfaces of other search engines, Google's user interface came as a welcome relief. It improved search times, worked better, and was easier to use.

3. An Expanding Community Google's search algorithm became well-known for producing high-quality results quickly. The number of people using Google to do their searches increased as a result of positive word of mouth and other factors.

4. Primary Capital Contribution Larry and Sergey successfully raised $100,000 from Sun Microsystems co-founder Andy Bechtolsheim in 1998. This injection of capital allowed them to properly incorporate Google as a corporation, obtain better hardware, and hire extra people.

5. The Release The year 2004 marked a watershed moment in Google's history, as that was the year the firm went public. The IPO was one of the greatest in terms of technology at the time, raising $1.67 billion.

As Google grew in popularity, it introduced new features and products. Google News, Google Maps, and Gmail all contributed to the company's growing dominance on the Internet.

Larry Page and Sergey Brin overcame early setbacks because of the lessons they learned and the fortitude they developed. Google's extraordinary success can be attributed to the company's founders' dedication to conquering challenges and providing customers with a superior search experience. Google has evolved from a simple search engine into a worldwide technology powerhouse, fundamentally altering the way in which we access and use information.

Chapter 2
Garage to Googleplex

2.1 One of the most influential technological businesses in the world had its roots in a garage where Google was founded. In an inconspicuous garage in Menlo Park, California, Google's visionary founders Larry Page and Sergey Brin began their adventure that would result in the company's rapid and extraordinary expansion.

In September 1998, Larry Page and Sergey Brin formally incorporated their search engine invention, which was originally called "Backrub." This is the beginning of the Google tale. They had borrowed space in a garage belonging to Susan Wojcicki, who would go on to play a pivotal role at Google. Google's first "real" workplace was a garage at 232 Santa Margarita Avenue.

The founders of Google were in their mid-20s, and their decision to operate out of a garage reflected their low funding and resources. It was a far cry from the palatial headquarters associated with computer firms today. Old wooden doors were used as desks and mounted on sawhorses in the modest garage.

Although Google had humble beginnings in a garage, Larry and Sergey were able to focus on their goal of creating a system to index all of the world's information and make it easily searchable and helpful to everyone. They put in a lot of time and effort to enhance their PageRank algorithm, make more precise search results, and increase the number of pages in their index.

The ethos of innovation and collaboration that permeated Google's garage in its early days is one of the most fascinating things about the company's origins. In order to advance search technology, Larry and Sergey encouraged interdisciplinary collaboration between engineers and computer scientists. As Google expanded, its distinctive culture of invention became an integral part of the company's identity.

Larry and Sergey's early struggles, such as meager finance and stiff competition from established search engines, only served to strengthen their resolve. Andy Bechtolsheim, co-founder of Sun Microsystems, invested $100,000 in the company, providing a significant boost that allowed them to acquire additional machinery and resources.

With a rising user base and a reputation for producing highly relevant search results, Google's rapid rise was evident. Google's search engine grew in popularity as word of mouth spread about how quickly and effectively it worked for its customers. Google swiftly surpassed its rivals and established its place in the IT industry.

Google outgrew its garage beginning in 1999 and relocated to more suitable quarters in Palo Alto, California. This event signified the transformation of the corporation from a fledgling enterprise to one with enormous potential.

The fact that Google was founded in a garage demonstrates the potential of creativity, hard work, and faith in a game-changing idea. Google's meteoric rise to the status of global technology powerhouse can be traced back to its co-founders, Larry Page and Sergey Brin, and their dogged pursuit of an improved method of searching the internet for relevant results. The garage where Google was founded still serves as a constant reminder of the company's dedication to improving the search experience for its users.

2.2 The earliest Google offices, staff, and culture were crucial in developing Google's unique character and setting the groundwork for the company's future success. When Google first began, it was a modest business with huge dreams, and the way it ran mirrored the ingenuity and teamwork that would come to define the company.

A garage at 232 Santa Margarita Avenue in Menlo Park served as the company's first official office. When Google was formally established in September 1998, this unremarkable building served as its headquarters. The garage was rented by Larry Page and Sergey Brin from their acquaintance Susan Wojcicki, who went on to play a pivotal role at Google.

The garage was small and unassuming in comparison to the massive campuses and cutting-edge buildings that Google is now famous for. Larry and Sergey's workstations were made from old wooden doors set on sawhorses. The room had only the most essential furnishings, which were a reflection of the company's tight finances and scarce resources at the time.

In spite of its austerity, Google's original headquarters was a hive of inventiveness and single-mindedness. It was an environment where new ideas were encouraged, and the founders and their initial small team of employees were committed to finding novel approaches to difficult issues in web search. The PageRank algorithm, which would eventually change the way web sites were ranked and searched, was developed and refined in the garage.

Early Google workers were mostly other computer scientists and engineers who believed in Larry and Sergey's mission to revolutionize the way people search the web. They were intrigued by the company's emphasis on intellectual curiosity and problem-solving, in addition to the promise of technical innovation. Employees were encouraged to use their critical thinking skills, challenge the status quo, and work together to find answers to problems because of the company's culture.

Google's team size and operational complexity expanded in tandem with its stellar reputation for providing reliable search results. In 1999, the company made the switch from garage to larger office space in Palo Alto, California, symbolizing the company's growth from startup to established business.

There were a few defining characteristics of the early Google culture that have persisted to this day:

Invention: 1. Google promoted an environment where employees felt safe trying new things and were rewarded for thinking creatively.

The organization had a meritocracy in which talent and results were given more weight than position. Ideas were evaluated independently of the speaker's position or seniority.

The founders of Google encouraged trust and teamwork among employees by keeping lines of communication open and transparent.

Fourth, a User-Centric Methodology: The satisfaction of its users has always been central to Google's purpose, and that hasn't changed.

5. Decision Making Based on Data Google's decision-making process relied heavily on data and analytics, a trend that continues to this day.

The early Google campus, its workers, and its culture are all a reflection of the company's dedication to innovation, collaboration, and a focus on the user. This groundwork was important in Google's growth from a garage startup to an international technology powerhouse that has and will continue to profoundly impact how people find, use, and share information online.

2.3 Google's brand history is remarkable because it shows the company's dedication to innovation, user-centric design, and a streamlined, minimalist style as it has grown. Since its founding in 1998, Google has undergone considerable branding changes, ultimately becoming one of the most recognizable and important technological businesses in the world.

The Beginnings (1998-2000) The evolution of the Google brand started with a single logo. The first Google logo, created in 1998 when Larry Page and Sergey Brin formed the company, featured a childlike script and primary colors. It was a direct reflection of the founders' original goal of making the service welcoming to newcomers. There was an anti-establishment, "Don't Be Evil" vibe to the early Google brand, which prioritized practicality over flare.

Symbolic History of the Google Logo, 2000-2015 In 2000, Google introduced a more polished and recognized logo that retained the core colors but featured a modest modification in font design. With this logo, we took our first move toward a more serious, corporate identity, while keeping our signature sense of humor and friendliness intact. During this time, Google's "Don't Be Evil" tagline began to emerge as an integral part of the company's brand.

Rebranding Google in 2015 (3): The new Google logo debuted in September 2015 as part of the company's comprehensive rebranding initiative. The new logo, which used a bespoke typeface dubbed "Product Sans," was designed to be easily recognized across a wide range of digital mediums. The replacement of "Don't Be Evil" with "Do the Right Thing" is another sign of Google's maturation as a company and its commitment to social responsibility.

During the Fourth Decade of the Alphabet Inc. In a dramatic corporate restructure in 2015, Google became a subsidiary of Alphabet Inc. Separating Google's main businesses like search and advertising from its other endeavors like driverless cars and bio sciences was the goal of this reorganization. Google's initial "Don't

Be Evil" mindset was further separated from the company's new branding.

5. Design and Brand Consistency in All Materials: Google's Material Design is a new design language with an emphasis on simplicity, vibrancy, and user friendliness. Users will have a uniform visual experience across all Google products thanks to the company's consistent use of this design language. Google's dedication to accessibility and user friendliness is shown in Material Design.

Google's Current Logo (Since 2015): The current Google logo is made up of the iconic "G" symbol and the word "Google" in a unique typeface that uses the same primary colors that have become synonymous with the brand. The new logo is simple, contemporary, and responsive, all of which pay homage to Google's widespread reach across all platforms.

7. Extending Your Brand New Google goods and services have been released over the years, each with its own logo and branding, but all sharing the same ethos. This has led to a wide range of products, from Gmail to YouTube, each of which has its own logo and design while still seeming like it belongs to the same family.

User-centered innovation, number eight: Google's brand development has always been linked to the company's emphasis on user-centered experimentation. Google's logo and other graphic elements are created to simplify and streamline the process of using the company's offerings.

In summary, the evolution of the Google brand is distinguished by a transition from its early, humorous logo to a more professional, corporate identity that places user experience and design consistency at the forefront. The brand evolved to reflect the dynamic nature of the technological and innovative world as Google added new products and reorganized its business. With its commitment to accessibility and user-centric design, Google has become more than just a search engine; it now represents a wide range of products and services.

Chapter 3
The Google Algorithm

3.1 Investigating the inner workings of Google's search algorithm uncovers the depth and complexity of one of the web's most vital components. Google's search algorithm lies at the heart of the company's ambition to organize the world's information and make it universally accessible and valuable. Learning its inner workings can shed light on the mysteries of internet research.

First, "Crawling and Indexing" Crawling and indexing the web are the first steps in Google's search algorithm. Google makes use of a massive network of web crawlers (sometimes called Googlebots or spiders) to find and classify new content on the World Wide Web. These automated programs crawl the web by following links and cataloging each page they see. Google's index is a huge database where the data is saved.

Algorithm for PageRank The PageRank algorithm, created by Larry Page and Sergey Brin while they were students at Stanford University, is the backbone of Google's search algorithm. PageRank is a link analysis tool that ranks websites by the quality and number of inbound connections. Pages with more high-quality inbound links are considered more authoritative and, consequently, get higher PageRank ratings.

3. New and Improved Algorithms Google's search algorithm is constantly being updated in an effort to provide ever-better results. Algorithm updates, also called "Google updates," are released with the goals of reducing spam, enhancing the user interface, and adjusting to new trends in both website material and user habits.

4. Signals for Ranking: Google's algorithm takes into account a wide variety of ranking signals when deciding where to place websites in search results. Off-page signals consist of things like backlinks, social signals, and brand authority, whereas on-page signals include things like keyword relevance, content quality, and user

experience, and technical features like page speed, mobile friendliness, and secure connections.

Machine Learning, number 5. Machine learning and AI are becoming increasingly integrated into Google's algorithm. In 2015, Google added a machine learning component called RankBrain, which improves the search engine's ability to understand and interpret user queries. It constantly adjusts the order of search results based on how users interact with them.

Query Context and User Intent, Number Six: Google's search algorithm makes an effort to deduce the user's intent and return results that are relevant to the question being asked. For instance, it recognizes the difference between searches seeking information, navigation, or a certain type of transaction, and responds accordingly.

7. Regional and Individual: Google's algorithm considers a user's location and customization settings. Personalized search results take into account a user's search history and preferences, while local search results focus on companies and services in the immediate area.

Indexing for mobile devices first With the rising use of mobile devices, Google announced mobile-first indexing in 2019. This emphasizes the significance of a website's mobile-friendly design, as the mobile version is the one most often used for ranking and indexing.

Expertise, authority, and trustworthiness (EAT) 9. When it comes to articles about health, finances, and similar taboo subjects, Google's algorithm places a heavy weight on the EAT principle. Search engines give more weight to content that is high-quality, well-researched, and authoritative.

10. Criminal Sanctions and Quality Standards If a website is found to be engaging in spamming methods or providing low-quality material, Google's algorithm will penalize the offending domain.

When penalized, a website's visibility in search results may drop or perhaps vanish altogether.

A complex and dynamic system, Google's search algorithm integrates technological procedures, AI, and a profound knowledge of user behavior and purpose. It prioritizes content quality, user experience, and best practices in order to provide the most relevant and informative search results to users. Website proprietors, digital marketers, and SEO experts who want to maximize their sites' exposure in search engine results must have a firm grasp of the inner workings of Google's search algorithm.

3.2 Larry Page and Sergey Brin's creation of PageRank is a pivotal moment in the growth of search engines and the way people find information on the web. To really appreciate PageRank, one must acknowledge the revolutionary changes it has wrought in search engine results, content relevance, and the online experience as a whole.

PageRank, at its heart, is an algorithm that provides a numerical value to web pages depending on the quality and amount of incoming links from other pages. There are a few main reasons why PageRank is so important:

Quality and Relevance 1. When it comes to web page rankings, PageRank added a whole new dimension. PageRank took into account the amount and quality of links going to a website rather than just the frequency with which keywords appeared on that website's content. Because of this shift in emphasis, search engine rankings now favor pages with higher-quality, more authoritative backlinks.

Confronting Internet Spam Web spam, low-quality material, and pages stuffed with keywords to manipulate ranks were commonplace before PageRank. The PageRank algorithm's reliance on external links made it more difficult for spammers to manipulate the system. In order to rise in search engine ranks, websites needed to obtain high-quality backlinks, which led to an increase in overall content quality.

Thirdly, a "Link-Based Citation System": PageRank can be considered as a link-based citation system for the web. In essence, it turned the entire web into a massive reference library where each connection between pages functions as a citation. Backlinks from respectable pages have the same effect on search engine rankings as citations from trustworthy sources do in scholarly work.

(4) User-centric relevance: This user-centric approach to relevance was made possible by the algorithm's emphasis on the web's innate structure of linkages, which effectively transformed web pages into

"votes" for other pages. Search results that had higher PageRank scores were more likely to provide useful information in response to users' inquiries.

Improved User Experience, Number 5. The reliability and high standard of search results were greatly enhanced by PageRank. A higher proportion of relevant results were returned to users. Because of this better search experience, Google gained popularity and users very quickly.

As Google developed internationally, the worldwide impact of PageRank became more apparent. Google's dedication to providing users with highly relevant and accurate results led to the company's meteoric rise to prominence as the world's preferred search engine. It was more than a simple search engine; it was the gateway to the internet's vast trove of data.

7. Contest and Innovation The advent of PageRank stimulated creativity and rivalry among search engines. It established a new benchmark for search engine technology, inspiring competitors to develop and improve their own algorithms to provide better results for users.

8. Monetization: PageRank helped Google make money off of contextual advertising in its search results. Google AdWords was born out of the observation that users were more likely to interact with and click on adverts when they were directly related to their search queries.

In conclusion, PageRank is groundbreaking because it shifted the emphasis of web search from keywords to the relevance and authority of inbound links. This new strategy changed search by making it more accurate, user-centric, and resistant to spam, ultimately paving the way for Google to become the leading search engine and an influential force in the digital environment. To this day, PageRank still has a profound effect on how the internet is organized and how we find information using search engines.

3.3 Search engines like Google can only exist because of constant work to improve their search algorithms. Search engines continually evolve to produce more accurate, relevant, and tailored results, adapt to changing user behavior and technical advances, and solve new difficulties, such as spam and misinformation. These actions are crucial to ensure that search engines continue to be useful for user engagement and information retrieval.

Some essential features of the ongoing work to improve search algorithms are as follows:

1. Feedback from Users and Quality Assessment: Clicks, page views, and user satisfaction surveys are only some of the user data collected and analyzed by search engines. Using this information, we may fine-tune our algorithms to produce outputs that better meet the requirements of our users. Search results are evaluated by quality raters to make sure they adhere to standards.

2. Algorithm Updates: Search engines, especially Google, issue algorithm updates on a regular basis. These changes are an attempt to combat issues like spam, poor quality content, and manipulated rankings while also increasing the relevancy and quality of search results. Some updates, like the Panda one that penalizes low-quality material and the Mobile-Friendly update that favors mobile-friendly sites, may have a more narrow focus.

AI and machine learning, third. Machine learning and artificial intelligence (AI) are being incorporated into the algorithms of search engines. As a result of these innovations, search results can be tailored to each individual user and their specific situation. Google's RankBrain, for example, employs machine learning to evaluate and comprehend complicated, ambiguous requests.

4. Natural Language (NLP): Understanding and deciphering human language in search queries has become increasingly reliant on NLP technology. Improvements in natural language processing (NLP) have allowed search engines to understand the nuance, context, and purpose of users' queries, yielding more relevant results.

Fifthly, Semantic Search Instead of relying merely on keywords, semantic search seeks to comprehend the meaning of words and their relationships in a query. This method improves the ability of search engines to match information to user searches, regardless of the exact wording of those inquiries.

Mobile-First Indexing, Number Six Web pages that are optimized for mobile use are given higher rankings in search results. Because of the significance of responsive design, mobile-first indexing prioritizes the mobile version of a website for ranking and indexing content.

Search engines take into account user experience cues like website speed, mobile friendliness, and secure connections to provide a better overall search experience. One of the most important goals of algorithm improvement is to guarantee a safe and frictionless experience for end consumers.

More and more attention is being paid by search engines to the problem of spreading false information. Search engines now incorporate fact-checking data and modify their algorithms to prioritize authoritative and reliable sites.

Voice Search and Local Search 9. Improvements have also been made to voice and localized search. Voice-assisted search experiences that comprehend natural language and context are being developed, and algorithms are working to present users with relevant results based on their location.

Privacy and data security come in at number ten. Algorithms must also consider privacy and data protection requirements. Users' private information is protected and processed in accordance with applicable laws.

The improvement of search algorithms is a continual and ever-changing process. To stay ahead of the competition, major search engines like Google spend a lot of time and money on R&D,

resulting in frequent changes and new features. In light of the challenges posed by the ever-evolving digital ecosystem, these initiatives strive to make web searching more user-centric and information-rich. More developments are on the horizon for search, ones that will further highlight the significance of user intent, quality content, and user trust.

Chapter 4
Competition and Collaboration

4.1 Early on, Google had to contend with a number of other search engines that also wanted a piece of the fast expanding internet search industry. However, Google was able to surpass its rivals and become the industry standard because of its novel strategy, cutting-edge technology, and unrelenting emphasis on user experience.

1. Yahoo: When Google first entered the search engine market, Yahoo was one of its initial competitors. Early versions of Yahoo's search engine had a directory-like structure, in which editors manually categorized websites. In contrast, Google's PageRank algorithm, which takes into account both the quality and amount of links, yields more precise and pertinent outcomes. Google's rapid expansion can be attributed to the fact that its users instantly recognized its improved search quality.

Alternate View: Popular in the late '90s, AltaVista was noted for its innovative tools and thorough search results. Google, on the other hand, stands out because of its focus on accuracy and ease of use. Google's layout is far simpler and easier to navigate than AltaVista's was, which was crowded with ads and other distractions. Google's success can be attributed in part to this design ethos.

 In addition to Google and Bing, Excite was a major player in the search engine industry. With Google's PageRank algorithm, users were guaranteed to see the most credible and pertinent search results possible. On the other hand, Excite used more basic keyword matching techniques. Google's technology provided it a major lead in offering superior search results.

4. Lycos: Lycos was one of the first search engines around, and it also dabbled with web portals. But Google won over people with its unrelenting commitment to search quality, relevance, and speed. One area in which Google stood out from the competition was in its ability to understand and respond to user intent.

HotBot: #5 While HotBot's search functions were more sophisticated than those of its competitors in the late '90s, Google's PageRank algorithm ultimately proved to be the deciding factor. Users felt more confident in the accuracy and usefulness of Google's results because they were grounded in the web's inherent link structure, which gave greater weight to reputable sources.

America Online (AOL) was a pioneer in the online world, and its search engine, AOL Search, is a throwback to those heady days. Its platform now includes AOL Search as well. AOL was only one of many major ISPs and browsers that partnered with Google because of its stellar reputation for providing relevant search results. Because of this, Google was able to reach a far wider audience.

Several important elements contributed to Google's early success:

"- PageRank Algorithm Google's ability to provide more accurate and relevant search results thanks to the PageRank algorithm was a major selling point that attracted people rapidly.

Users who were sick of fumbling through complicated search engine results pages found solace in Google's uncluttered interface and its emphasis on providing a quick and effective search experience.

 New ideas: Google was able to maintain its dominance in the ever-evolving search scene thanks to its commitment to constant innovation in areas such as machine learning, enhanced algorithms, and personalized search results.

Partnerships in Business Google's expansion was aided by the strategic alliances it struck with major ISPs and browser developers.

- Brand Trust: Google's commitment to user privacy and high-quality search results, as well as its "Don't Be Evil" mantra, have earned the trust of users and boosted the company's reputation.

Ultimately, Google's continuous pursuit of innovation and its focus on user-centric design, along with its innovative PageRank algorithm, helped it to surpass its early competitors and become the dominant force in the world of search engines. Google has expanded beyond its original mission as a search engine to become a multifaceted technology company whose offerings have revolutionized the way we use the internet.

4.2 Google's expansion and development have been greatly aided by strategic alliances; mergers with Yahoo and AOL, for example, had a profound effect on the company's trajectory in the early 2000s. These relationships allowed Google to increase its reach, cement its leadership in the search business, and broaden its user base. Let's talk about the most significant alliances and their effects:

1. Yahoo's 2000 partnership:

One of the most well-known names on the web at the time, Yahoo, joined forces with Google in a strategic collaboration in the year 2000. Yahoo's search engine is now powered by Google's search technology thanks to the deal between the two companies. The results of this collaboration were numerous:

Expansion of the Market: Google benefited from Yahoo's massive user base by becoming Yahoo's search engine provider.

To Generate Income: Google was able to increase its income thanks to its agreement with Yahoo. Yahoo compensated Google for the use of its search technology, adding to Google's financial development.

Yahoo's adoption of Google's search technology boosted both the company's and Yahoo's profile as a top search engine provider.

- Reliable Users: Users' faith in Google's search abilities was bolstered by the company's collaboration with Yahoo, which is known for its own high-quality search results.

AOL's Co-Operation in 2002:

A major relationship between Google and AOL was established in 2002. As part of this collaboration, Google invested $1 billion into AOL, giving it a 5% interest in exchange for Google's services. This transaction had a major effect:

Increased Market Share: Google's purchase in AOL allowed it to secure a dominant position in the market. Since many people were already using AOL Search, Google's partnership with them helped the search engine dramatically increase its market share.

Advertisement Dissemination: Google secured an exclusive contract to serve as AOL's sole provider of search and contextual advertising across all of AOL's assets as part of the deal. This increased Google's ad exposure and revenue even more.

- More Money Coming In: Google's position as an industry leader in internet advertising was strengthened by the exclusive ad distribution agreement.

Expansion of the User Base: Google's user base grew substantially as a result of their collaboration with AOL. Google's search engine and advertising platforms were made available to millions of AOL users, which aided in the company's rise to prominence in the search industry.

Google's rise to prominence in the search and advertising industries was aided by strategic alliances with Yahoo and AOL. Google's revenue, brand recognition, and proportion of the market were all boosted as a result of these partnerships. Users who participated in these agreements reacted positively to Google's reputation for providing high-quality search results and its dedication to user experience, further solidifying Google's status as the go-to search engine.

While these collaborations had a significant impact, Google's long-term success hinged on the company's dedication to innovation, user-centric design, and the enhancement of its search algorithms. Over the years, Google continued to grow and broaden its services, becoming a worldwide computer juggernaut that stretches far beyond its search engine roots.

4.3 Changes in technology, consumer tastes, and the cutthroat nature of the online marketplace have all contributed to the current state of the search engine environment. There has been a shift in how people use search engines, and this parallels how people use the internet generally. Some of the most noteworthy changes are discussed here.

The Growth of Google 1. The rise of Google in the late 1990s and early 2000s had a profound effect on the competitive landscape of search engines. By placing a premium on both relevancy and usability, Google's PageRank algorithm completely changed the search landscape. Its organic-focused design and streamlined aesthetic are groundbreaking.

Market Consolidation and Increasing Competition Google may be the most well-known search engine, but it has plenty of rivals. Microsoft's Bing has become a serious challenger thanks to its novel approach to search. Privacy- and sustainability-oriented search engines are also available, such as DuckDuckGo and Ecosia. However, market consolidation is typical of the search industry, with Google holding a major share of the market.

 Mobile and voice search have gained prominence due to the popularity of smartphones and digital assistants. Google and other search engines have modified their interfaces and algorithms to better serve customers who conduct searches using voice commands and mobile devices.

Semantic Search, Number 4. Understanding the context and intent of search queries has grown increasingly crucial, and semantic search technology has played a key role in this. Instead than just matching keywords, it takes into account the context in which those keywords are used. Google's "Hummingbird" algorithm update in 2013 marked a key step in this approach.

Five, Customization: Today's search engines are smart enough to tailor their results based on a user's past queries, current location, and other personal details. The goal of this customization is to deliver more relevant search results for each individual user.

Sixth, Artificial Intelligence and Machine Learning: Artificial intelligence (AI) and machine learning are currently used by search engines to better grasp user intent, provide more relevant results, and interpret contextual information. For instance, Google's RankBrain makes use of machine learning to improve search results.

Search Engines That Target a Specific Industry or Topic7. YouTube for videos, Amazon for goods, and LinkedIn for business connections are just a few examples of the rise in popularity of niche search engines. Users' reliance on these sites for niche information makes them formidable competitors in the search market.

Visual and picture searches can now be conducted with the use of search engines. Users now have a new option for finding relevant results when conducting a search.

The Local Search Nine Users increasingly prioritize local search results while looking for goods and services. Search engines have evolved to return results relevant to a user's immediate vicinity.

Privacy and data security come in at number ten. There has been a shift toward safeguarding individuals' personal information and privacy. Increasing user awareness of data usage has inspired new privacy-centric search engines like DuckDuckGo.

Problems posed by false information and propaganda Fighting false information and hoaxes is a difficult task for search engines. When checking facts, algorithms are tweaked to prioritize reputable sources.

Expansion Around the World: Search engines now cover a wider geographical area, offering results in a variety of languages and focusing on a wider range of international consumers.

The dynamic character of the digital age is reflected in the ever-changing landscape of search engines. Innovation, shifting user expectations, and the pursuit of better search quality and relevance characterize this era. Search engines' centrality in providing access to relevant information and influencing how we find and use content in the modern web is undeniable.

Chapter 5
The Dot-Com Bubble

5.1 During the dot-com bubble, which lasted from about 1997 to 2000, Google had a number of difficulties as well as possibilities. After a period of fast expansion and speculative investment in internet-based businesses, the "dot-com bubble" promptly burst. Google, which launched in 1998, was a young company amid a tumultuous period for the IT sector.

1. Origin and Rapid Expansion, 1998–1999: Google was founded by Larry Page and Sergey Brin while they were Ph.D. students at Stanford University. The company was founded in September 1998 with the goal of making all of the world's knowledge easily searchable and helpful to everyone. Google's humble beginnings may be traced back to a garage in Menlo Park, California, where a small group of people worked. At its height, the dot-com boom saw innumerable internet firms raise hundreds of millions of dollars.

Second, Financing Difficulties: Google has a tough time getting started due to finance issues. Due to the speculative character of the dot-com bubble, many investors poured money into various internet enterprises, even if they had no obvious route to profitability. Investors seeking fast revenue growth were less interested in Google because of its emphasis on technology, algorithm improvement, and search quality.

Google, in contrast to many other firms of its day, grew slowly and steadily. Rather of actively pursuing new investors, the firm concentrated on honing its search algorithm and increasing the reliability of search results. By concentrating on its flagship product, Google set the stage for sustained growth.

Four, The Initial Expenditure: In August of 1998, Andy Bechtolsheim, co-founder of Sun Microsystems, wrote a check for $100,000 to Google. This was the company's first major investment.

With the money from this investment, Google was able to buy the equipment it needed to expand.

AdWords was first introduced in 2000. In October of 2000, Google introduced its advertising platform known as AdWords. In spite of the bursting of the dot-com bubble, this was a major step toward monetization. AdWords allowed advertisers to bid on keywords and display text ads alongside search results, establishing a successful business model that would later become one of Google's principal sources of income.

Getting Through the "Dot-Com" Crash of '00-'01: Google's search engine technology and user base both improved and grew throughout the dot-com meltdown, when many rivals went out of business. The company was able to weather the storm thanks to its methodical approach to growth and its concentration on search quality.

7. Expansion After the Dot-Com Bust, 2002–2004: Google's growth has been consistent since the bursting of the dot-com bubble. Revenue and user growth were propelled by its cutting-edge advertising platform and unwavering dedication to providing useful search results. Google's Initial Public Offering (IPO) in 2004 was a major turning point in the company's history and cemented its standing as a preeminent technology enterprise.

Google's perseverance and dedication to providing a first-rate search experience distinguished the company throughout the dot-com bubble. Google was able to emerge as a dominant force in the tech industry in the years following the bubble, which was characterized by hype, speculative investments, and the subsequent crash. This was made possible by the company's focus on core technology, its more conservative approach to funding, and its dedication to user-centric innovation. This event played a crucial influence in developing Google's long-term success and its position as one of the world's most prominent technological businesses.

5.2 Several important methods, concepts, and practices set Google distinct from many of its contemporaries, allowing it to endure and grow in a tumultuous market, especially during the dot-com bubble and its aftermath. The following elements contributed to Google's success in the face of a highly competitive and often unstable industry:

Prioritize Basic Research and Development: Google has always put great emphasis on its search engine's performance and reliability. Google invested heavily in refining its search algorithms to ensure consumers received accurate and relevant search results while many dot-com startups chased quick revenue growth without a clear route to profitability. Google's dedication to fundamental technologies is what made the company indispensable.

Quantifiable Development Google, in contrast to many dot-com-era firms, took a measured and long-term approach to expansion. The company properly managed its spending and didn't rush into aggressive financing or expansion for the sake of speedy growth. Google was able to escape the problems of over-leveraged and over-extended businesses because to this strategy.

Monetization Plan No. 3: In 2000, Google launched its advertising platform called AdWords, which provided a novel and efficient means of generating income for the company. Google established a reliable revenue stream when it started letting businesses bid on keywords and show text advertising next to search results. One of the company's main sources of income is now derived from this novel approach to advertising.

Fourth, a User-Centric Methodology: Users have faith in and devotion to Google because of the company's commitment to providing relevant search results and a pleasant experience. The firm's founders were motivated by a desire to "organize the world's information and make it universally accessible and useful." The value of the customer's experience was stressed by this goal-oriented strategy.

5. Future Prospects Google's Larry Page and Sergey Brin started the company with an eye toward the future. They were not just focused on short-term financial advantages but on establishing a lasting and profound impact on the internet and how people access information. Because of this foresight, Google was able to maintain its dedication to its founding ideas despite the upheaval in the market.

The ability to change and improve Google constantly spent money on R&D and was open to innovative ideas. The company was ahead of the curve in its implementation of machine learning and AI, which led to more precise search results and user customization.

Services Diversification 7. Google has diversified its offerings over time to include more than just search, with the introduction of products like Gmail, Google Maps, Google Drive, and Android. The company was able to expand its customer base and strengthen its foothold in several different technology markets as a result of this strategy shift.

Google's expansion into new markets throughout the world is a key factor in the company's success. The company gave search results in numerous languages, adapted to local markets, and created a significant international presence.

Corporate accountability and integrity 9 Google's success can be attributed in part to the company's dedication to corporate responsibility and ethics. The "Don't Be Evil" slogan was used to stress the company's commitment to doing the right thing and earning the trust of its customers and business associates.

Strategic alliances and mergers are ten. To improve its offerings and increase its reach, Google has made a number of major acquisitions and developed partnerships. The company's success may be traced in large part to its strategic acquisitions, such as YouTube and Android.

Google's perseverance and success in the face of a volatile market can be traced back to the company's dedication to user-centered ideals, innovation, and a long-term vision. The company was able to weather the difficulties of the dot-com bubble thanks to its methodical approach to expansion, sustainable monetization model, and service diversification.

5.3 A major turning point in Google's development occurred on August 19, 2004, when the business went public with its Initial Public Offering (IPO). Google's founders, investors, and the IT industry as a whole all felt the effects of the company's IPO in various ways. Here, we underline the significance of the choice to go public:

One major benefit of Google's IPO was the increased access to finance it gained by offering shares to the general public. This flood of capital gave the company with the financial resources needed to fund its ambitious expansion ambitions, invest in research and development, and expand its services and infrastructure.

2. Founder and Early Investor Access to Funding The IPO provided Larry Page and Sergey Brin and other early investors and workers with a way to cash in their shares of Google. They were able to capitalize on their investments in the business by transforming their shares of ownership into publicly traded stock.

Google's popularity and respectability both rose dramatically after it went public. As a result of being subject to disclosure requirements and regulatory norms, the company became more transparent and accountable. This increased confidence and trust among customers and suppliers.

Incentives for Workers: Employee stock options and equity incentives were made possible by Google's initial public offering. By doing so, the company was able to connect the interests of its most valuable employees with the long-term profitability of the business.

Value to the Public Fifth: In light of investor emotions and expectations, the IPO set Google's public market valuation. Mergers and acquisitions, stock-based pay, and industry benchmarking were all affected by this value.

Possibilities for Growth and Mergers and Acquisitions With the money it raised from its initial public offering (IPO), Google was able to pursue novel growth prospects and make strategic acquisitions.

The company was able to diversify its offerings and enter new areas thanks to a number of strategic acquisitions.

The initial public offering (IPO) gave early investors access to a liquid market for selling their shares. The early Google backers who benefited from this were able to recoup their initial contributions.

8. Improved Regulatory Watching After going public, Google had to comply with stricter financial reporting, securities law, and corporate governance regulations. This aided in laying the groundwork for a corporation with a framework that promotes accountability and integrity in business.

9 Constant Performance Pressures: Since Google is a publicly traded corporation, it was expected that quarterly profits would be at least as high, if not more. The company's strategic decisions and its public relations were affected by this pressure.

Tendencies of Investors: After going public, Google had to satisfy a far more diverse group of stockholders. The corporation has to strike a balance between satisfying these stakeholders and staying true to its founding principles of long-term innovation and global information organization.

To get access to cash, provide liquidity for stakeholders, and solidify Google's position in the technology industry, the business made the historic decision to go public. It provided benefits, such as greater transparency and regulatory scrutiny, but it also brought difficulties, such as the pressure to live up to the expectations of investors. Despite these obstacles, Google was able to develop, diversify, and leave an indelible mark on the tech industry and the wider digital landscape thanks to its first public offering.

Chapter 6
Beyond Search: Google's Expanding Universe

6.1 Google's strategic diversification into areas beyond search, such as Gmail, Maps, and YouTube, has not only bolstered the company's position in the IT industry, but also improved the online lives of people all over the world. Google's growth and diversification into new areas have allowed the company to become deeply embedded in people's lives and routines.

1. Gmail:

Google's first step into the realm of electronic mail came in 2004 with the launch of Gmail. Gmail's revolutionary features, like ample free storage, effective spam filtering, and threaded chats, led to its rapid rise to prominence. The debut of Gmail signaled a revolution in how email services were supplied, delivering a more user-centric approach and transforming the way individuals manage their email. As other Google products, such as Google Drive and Google Calendar, have been increasingly integrated with Gmail, it has become indispensable for both personal and business use.

Google Maps, Number Two:

The release of Google Maps in 2005 marked a watershed moment in the history of global exploration and navigation. Google Maps' location-based services, in-depth street views, and real-time traffic updates have made it an invaluable tool for tourists, merchants, and commuters alike. Google's mapping service is one of the best since the company consistently invests in GIS and other mapping technologies. Google Maps is utilized for more than just getting about; it's also a portal for learning about nearby establishments, reading customer feedback, and uncovering hidden gems.

(3) On YouTube:

Google's acquisition of YouTube in 2006 signaled a substantial move into the area of internet video sharing. YouTube now dominates the online video space, with its huge catalog of amateur and professional videos as well as its support for live broadcasts. The platform has ushered in a new era of digital content production by facilitating communication between artists and consumers all around the world. With the help of Google's advertising network, YouTube has become a major source of income for the firm. In addition, YouTube is now a major cultural and educational influence in many fields, including film, politics, and education.

Android Number Four:

When Android by Google was released in 2008, it completely changed the mobile landscape. Android has quickly become the dominant mobile platform, utilized by the vast majority of smartphones and tablets worldwide. Google's reach and ability to provide a consistent digital experience across platforms have both been greatly enhanced by its incorporation into the mobile ecosystem. Google Play, the app marketplace, is built on Android as well, making it possible to distribute Android apps and apps that work with other Google services.

Google Drive, Number Five:

Google Drive, released in 2012, is Google's online storage and collaboration platform. It provides a place to keep and access digital media like photos, movies, and documents, and it works seamlessly with other Google products. With Google Drive, team members can work together in real time on documents, presentations, and spreadsheets, increasing output and accessibility. Google Drive has become an indispensable resource for both consumers and organizations because to its convenient accessibility from any device with an internet connection.

Google's objective is to make information accessible and helpful for everyone, thus the company's development into these many product offerings is in line with that goal. It has helped Google meet the needs of a broader audience and maintain its position as a major player in the technology sector. Additionally, the integration of these products into the Google ecosystem has produced a seamless and linked digital experience for users, confirming Google's position as a tech giant that defines how we communicate, navigate, and access information in the modern world.

6.2 Google's strategy of growth and expansion through acquisitions and investments has been essential in the company's ability to expand its product offerings and maintain its position at the forefront of innovation. Over the years, Google has expanded into new markets, improved current products, and pushed technological boundaries in large part by acquiring innovative startups and well-established enterprises in a wide range of fields. In this article, we'll look at some of Google's most famous investments and purchases:

To begin: 1. YouTube (2006) In a historic leap into the realm of Internet video sharing, Google paid $1.65 billion in stock to acquire YouTube. Since its inception, YouTube has rapidly grown to become the most popular video-sharing website in the world. The acquisition has also incorporated YouTube into Google's advertising network, earning significant revenue.

Second, Android from 2005: The Android operating system had its beginnings in 2005, when Google purchased Android Inc. Since then, Android has exploded in popularity, powering the vast majority of smartphones and tablets around the world. With this purchase, Google has solidified its position in the mobile industry.

Thirdly, DoubleClick in 2007: DoubleClick, a digital marketing firm, was purchased by Google for $3.1 billion. Google's ability to provide advertising solutions across multiple mediums, including display, video, and mobile, was bolstered by this purchase.

4. Waze (2013): Approximately $1.1 billion is how much Google paid to acquire Waze, a GPS navigation and traffic app. Google Maps now incorporates Waze's real-time traffic data and crowd-sourced navigation features, making both more useful to users.

Nest Labs, a developer of smart home technologies, was acquired by Google for $3.2 billion. Google was able to penetrate the burgeoning smart home industry with devices like the Nest thermostat and the Nest Secure security camera thanks to this acquisition.

DeepMind (2014), number six: The artificial intelligence business DeepMind was purchased by Google for a reported $600 million. Google's AI research has been greatly aided by DeepMind's knowledge of artificial intelligence and machine learning, which has found use in fields as diverse as healthcare and robotics.

Seventh, Fitbit (2021) For $2.1 billion, Google purchased Fitbit, a maker of wearable fitness tracking devices. With this purchase, Google hoped to increase its offerings in the wearables and fitness tracking markets and solidify its position as a leader in the health and wellness industry.

Waymo (formerly known as the Google Self-Driving Car Project): Google's investment in autonomous driving technology led to the formation of Waymo, a subsidiary of Alphabet Inc. (Google's parent company). Waymo was an early leader in the field of autonomous vehicle technology and the creation of self-driving cars.

Nineteen (13) Boston Dynamics: Boston Dynamics, a robotics company noted for its cutting-edge designs and discoveries in the field, was recently acquired by Google. Despite Google's interest in robotics and automation, the company sold Boston Dynamics to SoftBank.

10. Serious Financial Commitment to AI Google has poured a lot of money into various AI and ML startups and research projects. Google's continued leadership in the AI industry can be attributed in large part to the company's extensive investments in the field.

Google has been able to expand into new markets, improve its existing product offerings, and lead the way in technological developments because to the money it has spent on acquisitions and investments. They have been a crucial element in the company's diversity and innovation, enabling Google to maintain its position as a leading tech behemoth. As a result of these strategic decisions, Google has been able to contribute to the advancement of technology beyond its core search engine, such as driverless vehicles, smart home gadgets, artificial intelligence research, and more.

6.3 Google's strategic approach of diversifying its portfolio has allowed it to grow beyond its original search engine business and into a worldwide computing behemoth with a wide variety of products and services. Google's diversification strategy is exemplified by its propensity to make investments and acquisitions in businesses that share its goal of making information accessible and valuable for everyone. In this article, we examine Google's efforts to spread its investment wings.

One, Marketing and Research: Search and advertising are at the heart of Google's business model. Google's advertising platform, which includes AdWords and AdSense, has become a significant revenue generator, even if search is still the company's lifeblood. The company is now able to branch out into other markets thanks to this source of income.

Services on the Cloud: Google Cloud delivers cloud computing, data storage, and developer tools. Google can now compete with other cloud service providers like AWS and Azure because to its strategy of diversity. The customers Google Cloud caters to range from small businesses to multinational corporations.

System Software for Mobile Devices: Google's entry into the mobile operating system industry came courtesy of the Android acquisition. Google has risen to prominence in the mobile industry thanks to the widespread adoption of its Android operating system on mobile devices.

(4) Tools and other Hardware: Pixel smartphones, tablets, the Nest smart speaker, and the Fitbit wearable fitness tracker are just some of the hardware goods that Google produces. Google intends for this suite of products to function together as one cohesive ecosystem for mobile and desktop consumers.

IoT and the Five-Star Smart Home: Google has diversified into the IoT with its purchase of Nest Labs and subsequent development of smart home products. Google promises to empower users with smart, networked devices that boost convenience and control in their homes.

Video and online streaming content, number six: With the purchase of YouTube in 2006, Google was able to corner the market on online video-sharing platforms. Since its inception, YouTube has grown into a major hub for both amateur and professional content creators, and it has become a substantial source of advertising revenue for Google.

7. Machine learning and artificial intelligence: Google has spent a lot of money on AI and machine learning development and study. Language translation, image identification, and voice assistants are just a few examples of the many new services enabled by artificial intelligence.

8. Driverless Cars: Google has been in the forefront of developing self-driving cars and autonomous vehicle technologies through its wholly owned subsidiary Waymo. The transportation sector as a whole is undergoing this sort of diversification.

9. Medical and Biological Research: Google's DeepMind subsidiary has focused on AI applications in healthcare, including the development of tools for medical imaging and disease diagnostics. This diversification intends to solve important difficulties in the healthcare system.

10. Resources for Learning and Increasing Efficiency: Gmail, Google Drive, and Google Classroom are just a few of the Google apps included in G Suite (now Google Workspace), Google's suite of productivity and educational apps. These resources see heavy rotation in classrooms and workplaces alike.

Eleventh Environmental Programs: Google has made gains in sustainability and environmental initiatives, such as pledging to power its data centers entirely with renewable energy and funding wind and solar power projects.

Innovation, strategic investments, and the identification and pursuit of new opportunities are all key factors in Google's portfolio diversification. It allows the corporation to avoid risks associated with overreliance on a particular product or sector and promotes Google as a versatile tech company that can satisfy the changing demands and expectations of consumers and companies. By combining its many offerings into a cohesive ecosystem, Google is reiterating its dedication to improving people' digital experiences across all areas of their lives.

Chapter 7
Google in the Spotlight

7.1 Google's massive popularity and clout in the IT sector have made it an integral part of the Internet and influenced how we use the Internet for research, communication, and entertainment. Concerns ranging from data privacy to commercial dominance have brought more public scrutiny and government attention along with this expanding influence. Here, we discuss the increasing impact and scrutiny of Google:

First, Dominance and Competition in the Market:

Concerns concerning unjust market dominance by Google's search engine have been voiced around the world. Critics claim that its market strength can impede competition and innovation. Legal actions and antitrust investigations have been initiated in several jurisdictions on concerns that Google's business practices in search and advertising have an anti-competitive effect.

Two, Concerns About Data Privacy

Google's services, such as search, email, and mobile devices, generate massive volumes of user data. This has prompted worries about user privacy and data sharing. Concerns about Google's data policies and the possibility of misuse or breaches have drawn criticism and regulatory attention.

Thirdly, customized experiences and echo chambers:

Google's algorithms tailor both search and content recommendations to the individual user, which can lead to "filter bubbles" in which people only see stuff that confirms their preconceived notions. This has spurred discussion on how echo chambers contribute to the dissemination of misinformation in public discourse.

Fourth, the Absolute Dominance of Online Ads:

The Google AdWords and AdSense advertising platforms are industry leaders. This dominance has led to attention over problems including ad targeting, privacy, and the company's control over the online advertising ecosystem.

Fifthly, censorship and content moderation:

Google's content filtering procedures and worries about censorship on YouTube and other platforms have drawn criticism. It has been difficult to strike a balance between free expression and the need to remove potentially dangerous or objectionable material.

Sixth: Taxes and Regulations:

Like many other international firms, Google has faced criticism for how it handles taxes and government regulation in different nations. The attention of tax authorities and policymakers has been drawn to allegations of tax avoidance and profit shifting.

Seventh, Political and Ethical Issues:

Google's influence extends to politics and ethics, with questions raised about its role in elections, government contracts, and contentious programs like Project Maven and Dragonfly. Many people are worried that the corporation isn't acting ethically or following its objective.

8. Proprietary Rights and Originality in Content:

Google's indexing and presentation of information from publishers and news organizations have led to disputes over copyright problems. Some publishers fear that Google's policies will make it harder for them to make money off of their work.

9 New Entrants and Mergers:

Concerns about anti-competitive behavior and the necessity for greater regulatory control have been expressed in light of Google's acquisition of several enterprises. For instance, the company has been under regulatory scrutiny because of its recent acquisition of Fitbit and possible future expansion into the wearables sector.

Tenthly, legal and regulatory challenges:

Antitrust authorities, privacy regulators, and government agencies all around the world have taken action against Google, including a slew of regulatory actions, lawsuits, and fines. These lawsuits could alter the company's procedures and the competitive landscape.

The increasing importance of Google and the public's interest in the company highlight the difficulties of running a tech giant in the modern Internet environment. The demand on the corporation to address issues of privacy, competition, content control, and ethical procedures is constant. Google has worked to adapt to and meet shifting public expectations, and the company often communicates with legislators and other interested parties to help it understand and adapt to the internet and technology landscape. As Google's clout grows, the company will be under increased scrutiny and will need to strike a balance between fostering creative solutions while also being responsible corporate citizens and in accordance with applicable laws.

7.2 Issues linked to privacy, antitrust, and data gathering have been at the center of public discourse and regulatory actions, with internet companies like Google under significant scrutiny in these areas. In this article, we examine Google's unique position in relation to the most pressing issues around privacy, antitrust, and data collection:

Concerns About Privacy

1. Collection of Data and Individualization: Google's search, email, and mobile services all contribute to a massive trove of customer data. While this information is helpful in tailoring services to individual users, it also raises questions about the breadth of data gathering and the possibility of abuse.

2 Consent and Openness: Users may not be aware of Google's complete data use, according to critics, and Google's data policies have been accused of lacking openness. The question of whether or not users give their informed consent to the collection and use of their personal data arises.

Thirdly, Data Security and Breach: Given the sensitive nature of the data Google stores, data breaches and security mishaps are legitimate causes for alarm. The business must take appropriate measures to safeguard user information against theft or hacking.

4. Retaining and Erasing Data: Google's data retention practices have sparked discussions about privacy and the right to be forgotten. Google must strike a balance between user requests for data deletion and legitimate business interests.

Issues of Monopolization and Competitiveness:

Google has a near monopoly on the internet search engine and digital advertising industries. Concerns regarding fair competition have been raised in light of this market strength, as smaller competitors may find it difficult to compete.

2) Internet Search Engine Pre-installing Google Search on Android devices, as one example of Google's search engine policies, has been criticized for allegedly limiting customer choice and possibly stifling competition. Because of this, several governments are conducting antitrust probes.

Marketing Prevalence 3. The Google Ads platform is a powerhouse in the digital advertising industry. There are worries about the company's dominance in the internet advertising ecosystem and how that would affect other players in the market.

4. Limitations on Alternative Service Providers Device makers and app developers have claimed that Google is restricting their freedom to use and promote alternative platforms. As a result, anti-competitive practices are under closer scrutiny from authorities.

Data Mining and Marketing:

One, "Personalized and Targeted Ads" Ad targeting on Google's advertising platform is primarily dependent on user information. While tailored advertising have the potential to be more successful, there are legitimate privacy and manipulation problems associated with them.

Second, Cookie Tracking: It's been a hotly debated topic whether or not third-party cookies should be used to monitor users' online activities. The advertising business and privacy organizations have conflicting opinions on Google's decision to eventually remove support for third-party cookies in Chrome.

Thirdly, a duopoly between Google and Facebook controls a sizable chunk of the digital advertising business (the "digital advertising duopoly"). The dominance of this duopoly has consequences for ad pricing and market competition.

Fourth, Privacy Regulations have established standards for how businesses must deal with customer information. Examples include the EU's General Data Protection Regulation (GDPR) and

California's Consumer Privacy Act (CCPA). Google must change its operations to conform to these rules.

Google is navigating these difficulties by continuing to respond to privacy concerns, take part in regulatory talks, and adjust its rules and procedures. The company understands the need to strike a balance between innovation and user protection, as seen by its dedication to user privacy and data security and its cooperation with regulatory organizations. As public opinion and legal frameworks shift, concerns about privacy, antitrust, and data gathering are likely to remain at the forefront of discussions about Google and the wider internet industry.

7.3 Google's response to privacy, antitrust, and data gathering concerns has included strategic shifts, policy shifts, and outreach to authorities, consumers, and stakeholders. The importance of addressing these issues to the company's brand, user trust, and regulatory compliance is not lost on management. We'll talk about Google's approaches to overcoming these problems here.

(1) Enhanced Security:

- Confidentiality Settings Google has launched features and tools that allow consumers to have more control over their data. Users have control over their data and can decide whether or not to have their activity tracked in order to receive personalized recommendations in the privacy settings.

Information Sharing: For greater data ownership and control, Google provides data portability capabilities that let users export their data from Google services.

In Private Browsing Mode: Google Chrome's Incognito Mode allows users to browse the web without their activity being saved in their browsing history. Users' anonymity is safeguarded by this new addition.

- Regional Management To ensure users have visibility and agency over the collection and use of their location data, Google has provided options that allow them to manage location tracking.

2. Adherence to Personal Information Protection Laws

We are in Compliance with GDPR In order to meet the requirements of the General Data Protection Regulation (GDPR) of the European Union, Google has made changes to its policies and practices.

- Privacy Shield Compliant In response to the California Consumer Privacy Act (CCPA), Google has implemented adjustments to its data handling methods to comply with the regulation's obligations respecting user data rights.

3. Discontinuing Use of Third-Party Cookies

Chrome Updates: Google's move to stop supporting third-party cookies in its Chrome browser is a big deal since it shows the company is taking privacy seriously. The goal of this change is to improve users' privacy while also fostering the growth of new technologies for advertising targeting and measurement.

Privacy Playground: To strike a better balance between user privacy and the interests of the advertising business, Google has proposed the Privacy Sandbox initiative.

Disclosure Reports: Google releases transparency reports on a regular basis, providing information about requests from governments for user data and content removal, among other things. This openness promotes dependability and responsibility.

- Instructional Materials Google has put resources into programs like "Privacy Checkup" and "Security Checkup," which help users better protect their personal information and online safety.

(5) Involvement in Regulatory Processes

Conversational Involvement Google is highly engaged in its interactions with government agencies and policymakers. The firm has offered its thoughts on the new legislation, highlighting the importance of well-defined and fair guidelines.

- Advocacy Efforts Google has engaged in lobbying efforts, aiming to establish legislation that respect the complexity of the tech industry while safeguarding users' rights and supporting innovation.

Open Source Projects, Number Six:

- Contributions to Open Source Google encourages a community-based approach to strengthening online privacy and security by actively participating in open source projects. The development of technologies that protect users' privacy, such as encryption and safe web browsing, are supported by the firm.

Google's efforts to resolve customer concerns and meet changing legal requirements are reflected in the company's replies to privacy, antitrust, and data gathering difficulties. When it comes to innovation, consumer trust, and privacy, the organization understands the significance of striking a balance. Google's strategy has shown that it is committed to navigating the ever-changing landscape of the digital industry while placing a premium on protecting user data and privacy, and it is expected to do the same as these concerns develop further.

Chapter 8
Alphabet Inc.: A New Chapter

8.1 Google's commitment to openness, innovation, and diversification were reflected in the founding of Alphabet Inc. and the company's subsequent reorganization. This was a calculated decision made to improve efficiency, simplify the organizational structure, and give each division more attention. Here, we explain how Google will change with the establishment of Alphabet Inc.

Background:

In August 2015, Google co-founders Larry Page and Sergey Brin announced the establishment of Alphabet Inc. The goal of this organizational shakeup was to divide Google's conventional operations from its more daring and innovative side projects. The name "Alphabet" was selected to represent the company's goal to "organize the world's information" across its many operations.

Principal Aims

The reorganization aimed to accomplish numerous things:

Clarity and openness come first. The original intent of creating Alphabet was to better communicate the breadth and depth of the company's holdings. It helped separate Google's core search and advertising operations from the company's other divisions.

Second, Center on Creativity Google's intention in forming Alphabet was to give its subsidiaries greater autonomy through the appointment of their own chief executive officers and management teams. The hope was that this would encourage creativity and quick decision making across departments.

Relations with Investors (3): It was hoped that the new organizational structure would help shareholders better understand how each division was doing. Google's "Other Bets" would be treated as a separate segment from the company's core companies in financial reporting.

The New Organization

After the reorganization, Alphabet Inc. now owns 100% of Google and appointed Sundar Pichai as Google's CEO. Alphabet expanded its responsibilities by becoming a holding company for a number of different companies. Alphabet appointed Larry Page as CEO and Sergey Brin as President.

An entirely new section, "Other Bets," was added to better organize Alphabet's many businesses and initiatives that fall outside of Google's core competencies. Healthcare, self-driving cars (Waymo), the biomedical sciences (Verily), city planning (Sidewalk Labs), and other cutting-edge endeavors were all represented.

Several major outcomes and effects resulted from the reorganization:

Alphabet might explore creative projects with a view toward long-term development after granting greater autonomy and unique leadership to its many business sectors.

Alphabet's financial disclosures improved transparency by revealing the successes and setbacks of Google's core businesses, as well as those of Other Bets, to investors.

3. Financial Support for New Ideas Subsidiaries of Alphabet, such as Waymo (self-driving cars) and Verily (life sciences), have maintained their pace of innovation since the company's inception. The setup improved their chances of attracting funding and partners from elsewhere.

4. Adaptability and Nimbleness: Alphabet was able to better respond to opportunities and overcome obstacles thanks to its reorganized company structure and the dynamic nature of the modern economy.

Google's readiness to adapt to the ever-changing technological world was on full display with the founding of Alphabet Inc. and the subsequent restructuring of the corporation. It allowed Google to continue its original aim of organizing information while also encouraging innovation and tackling fresh problems in the IT sector. Alphabet Inc.'s well-defined organizational structure reaffirms the company's dedication to pursuing innovative solutions across a wide range of industries.

8.2 The logic behind Google's rebranding as Alphabet Inc. was crystal clear, and it included the company's dedication to organizational transparency, strategic focus, and the promotion of innovation. The company's operations, investor relations, and pursuit of lofty goals were all affected significantly by these shifts.

Rationale:

Clarity and openness come first. The reorganization was undertaken to better define roles and responsibilities inside the company. Alphabet was created to provide a clearer picture of Google's resource allocation and the performance of its various business areas by separating Google's core operations from its more experimental efforts.

Strategic Emphasis 2: Alphabet's formation gave its subsidiaries and other endeavors greater autonomy. Alphabet's divisions, including Google, each had its own chief executive officer and management group. The goal of giving each business unit more autonomy was to encourage a heightened focus on innovation and the unique requirements of each market.

3. Flexibility and Variability Rapid transformation and game-changing discoveries are hallmarks of the technology sector. The transformation was prompted by a desire to build a more agile organizational structure that could react to changing market dynamics and allocate resources more efficiently to handle growing opportunities and challenges.

4. Relations with Investors It is possible that Alphabet's financial reports will be more informative if Google's main businesses are reported separately from its "Other Bets" category. The goal was to give potential investors a clearer picture of the financial situation and future prospects of the numerous subsidiary enterprises.

Implications:

1 Innovation and experimentation: The reorganization at Alphabet made room for more experimentation. Startups like Waymo, Verily, and Sidewalk Labs were born out of the "Other Bets" category, and they've since made significant contributions to the advancement of autonomous vehicles, life sciences, and city planning. Even though some "Other Bets" were facing substantial financial issues, the more focused environment encouraged their inventions.

Allocation of Resources The degree to which resources might be allocated freely increased. Alphabet has the option to better distribute its resources throughout its divisions according to their respective performance and potential. The company was better able to seize opportunities and deal with threats as a result of this.

Thirdly, Investor Awareness The company's financial performance was broken down more specifically for the benefit of investors. Because of this openness, they were better able to gauge the future prospects for various business sectors and the overall health of the company's finances.

By reorganizing, Alphabet demonstrated its continued dedication to the future. The corporation was able to continue pursuing ambitious projects and taking on complicated global challenges by giving its subsidiary businesses more freedom to operate and allocating resources based on long-term objectives.

5. Impact on Regulations: Regulators, especially those concerned about antitrust issues, looked closely at Alphabet's corporate structure. Concerns about the company's market power and monopoly were voiced in light of its extensive subsidiary network and dominant position in internet search and advertising. The activities and prospective legal proceedings of the corporation were affected by this regulatory scrutiny.

Overall, a strategic ambition to preserve innovation, transparency, and organizational agility drove Google's rebranding as Alphabet

Inc. This enables Alphabet to continue "organizing the world's information" and to pursue high-risk endeavors with the potential to revolutionize entire industries and solve pressing global problems. However, the company's strategic decisions and interactions with its stakeholders have been and will continue to be influenced by the regulatory and competitive obstacles it has faced since the transformation began.

8.3 Parent business Alphabet Inc. oversees a wide variety of subsidiaries that specialize in various fields. These affiliates function autonomously to promote creativity and provide solutions to a wide range of international problems. Some of Alphabet's notable affiliates are discussed here.

1. Google: - Google remains a core subsidiary and represents the well-known search engine, advertising platform, and suite of services like Gmail, Google Maps, and Google Drive. It is at the forefront of Alphabet's operations and plays a critical role in the company's revenue generating.

Second, Waymo, a division of Google that specializes in transportation technology, has made great strides in the field of self-driving cars. It provides transportation services in certain areas and has branched out into logistics and driverless deliveries.

3. Verily: - Verily, formerly known as Google Life Sciences, is focused on healthcare and life sciences. In addition to health data analysis, clinical studies, and medical device development, the company also works on other cutting-edge initiatives. Verily has achieved significant strides in the fields of health research and disease prevention.

DeepMind is a research firm that studies the intersection of deep learning and AI. It has made important contributions in sectors like healthcare (using AI for early disease diagnosis) and gaming (creating AI capable of mastering complex games like Go).

5. Loon: Loon is a company well-known for its work on providing internet access via balloons. It has attempted to use high-altitude balloons equipped with communication gear to bring internet connectivity to underserved and distant areas.

Sidewalk Labs, at number six, is dedicated to bettering cities and fostering new forms of urban innovation. The firm investigates how to better utilize technology in urban infrastructure and residential areas in order to develop smart, sustainable communities.

Chronicle is a subsidiary of a cybersecurity company that provides analytics and detection for online threats. It offers services and resources to help businesses stay safe against cyberattacks.

8. X: - X (formerly Google X) is an incubator for groundbreaking ideas. Project Loon, Waymo, and Wing, a drone delivery service, are just a few of its most well-known endeavors.

9. Wing: - Wing is an autonomous delivery subsidiary that has developed delivery drones to speedily and efficiently transfer things to clients. The project's primary objective is to enhance methods of final-mile distribution.

Among Alphabet's other subsidiary companies is Chronicle, which focuses on identifying cybersecurity threats. It provides cutting-edge methods of identifying and counteracting security risks.

Alphabet's dedication to researching numerous technology developments and solving intricate international problems is reflected in its several subsidiary companies. The breadth of these divisions exemplifies the company's commitment to innovation, information organization, and positive societal and economic effect.

Due to Alphabet's organizational setup, these divisions can function autonomously while yet drawing on the parent company's resources and knowledge. It fosters an environment where groundbreaking ideas can be pursued and where technology can be leveraged to revolutionize different parts of daily life, from transportation and healthcare to internet connectivity and urban planning. Subsidiary companies play an important role in influencing the future of innovation and industry disruption as Alphabet continues to navigate the ever-changing tech landscape.

Chapter 9
The Innovations of Tomorrow

9.1 Google's forays into promising new areas, such as autonomous vehicles and artificial intelligence, have been game-changers. These initiatives showcase the firm's dedication to innovation and the creation of cutting-edge technology with the potential to revolutionize people's day-to-day lives, workplaces, and communities throughout the globe.

Google's foray into autonomous vehicles spawned Waymo, an Alphabet company. Waymo's contributions to the development of autonomous car technology have been crucial in shaping the transportation landscape of the future.

Important New Facts:

Early Advances 1. By 2010, Google has created a fleet of autonomous Toyota Priuses after first experimenting with the technology in 2005. Waymo's growth could not have been possible without these pioneering technologies.

(2) "Spin off" into "Waymo": Waymo was created as a separate entity from Google in 2016 to handle the company's autonomous vehicle research and development. Since then, Waymo's research and development efforts have been directed toward autonomous vehicle hardware and software.

The Third-Party Transportation App: Waymo has begun offering trips via ride-hailing in certain areas, with the journeys being fully autonomous. It was a major step forward in the process of making autonomous driving systems available to the general public.

Logistics and Shipping Waymo's uses have broadened from transportation of passengers to logistics and distribution. It's forming alliances with logistics firms and developing autonomous delivery systems.

Waymo prioritizes safety above everything else and has driven millions of miles autonomously in a wide range of settings to hone its technology.

Research into DeepMind and other forms of artificial intelligence:

Google's subsidiary DeepMind has made significant advancements in artificial intelligence (AI) technology, demonstrating the company's dedication to AI research and development.

Important New Facts:

New Developments in Deep Learning Google's AI work has significantly advanced machine learning and other AI applications by pushing the limits of deep learning.

2. Medical Software Medical image analysis, early disease diagnosis, and optimizing patient care are all areas in which DeepMind has applied AI.

DeepMind's AI systems have beaten human champions at games like Go and StarCraft II, marking a huge milestone in the field of gaming and artificial intelligence.

Using AI Everyday (4): Google's AI technologies are embedded across a wide range of the company's offerings, including language translation, image recognition, and voice assistants, all of which improve the user experience.

Google has participated in numerous conversations concerning the development of ethical AI, including the elimination of bias in AI algorithms and the establishment of guidelines for the conduct of ethical AI studies.

The consequences of Google's work in autonomous vehicles and AI span a wide range of sectors. The introduction of autonomous vehicles could significantly improve transportation for everyone.

They can help people with mobility issues or those who are elderly or disabled avoid accidents and reduce traffic congestion.

Google's advancements in the field of artificial intelligence are changing the way people engage with digital resources. With the promise to increase decision-making, user experiences, and the resolution of complicated problems, machine learning and deep learning approaches are altering industries such as healthcare, gaming, and language processing.

Google's focus to responsible innovation, which is becoming increasingly important as AI technologies grow more embedded into our daily lives, is further bolstered by the company's dedication to ethical AI development.

These initiatives show Google's dedication to technological innovation and its desire to bring about a future in which self-driving cars and AI-driven technologies help make the world a better, more efficient, and more interconnected place. The effects on numerous sectors and on society as a whole are anticipated to be far-reaching as Google continues to develop and expand these emerging technologies.

9.2 Alphabet Inc.'s DeepMind and Waymo's autonomous vehicle development efforts could have far-reaching consequences in the future of AI and transportation. These businesses represent ground-breaking innovations with the potential to completely alter whole industries and transform the way we live, work, and interact with technology.

DeepMind:

DeepMind is Google's artificial intelligence (AI) research division, and it focuses on creating cutting-edge machine learning and AI tools. It has embarked on numerous projects that could have far-reaching effects in many fields:

Innovations in Healthcare 1. DeepMind has been at the forefront of applying AI to healthcare. Artificial intelligence algorithms developed by the company have shown extraordinary performance in medical picture processing, facilitating the early diagnosis of conditions including diabetic retinopathy and breast cancer. This technology has the potential to enhance future healthcare delivery by lowering costs, speeding up diagnostics, and even saving lives.

2. Optimization of Patient Care Medical facilities have implemented DeepMind's AI technology to better serve their patients. These computers can analyze huge volumes of patient data to spot patterns and give doctors useful information, resulting in better, more individualized treatment.

Achievements in Gaming 3. The success of DeepMind's AlphaGo artificial intelligence system against the world's best Go player garnered headlines. The great potential of AI to tackle difficult challenges and excel at strategic games was on full display in this accomplishment.

DeepMind has participated in numerous conversations about how to create ethical AI. The importance of justice, openness, and accountability are emphasized in its principles for responsible AI research and its efforts to overcome biases in AI algorithms.

Medical care, video games, and the ethics of artificial intelligence could all benefit from DeepMind's work. They hold the potential for better AI-based medical diagnosis, enhanced patient care, and fresh takes on old challenges.

Waymo:

Waymo is Alphabet's autonomous driving division. Future transportation and logistics may be drastically altered by its innovations.

1) Self-Driving Cars and Ride-Hailing Services: Waymo is now offering autonomous rides to the general public through a commercial ride-hailing service. This app could revolutionize the transportation network company business by facilitating the widespread use of autonomous vehicles.

Waymo is being used for logistics and driverless deliveries. Self-driving cars have the potential to transform the logistics business by reducing delivery times and costs.

Thirdly, Efficiency and Safety: Potentially eliminating human error as a contributing factor in traffic accidents is a major goal of self-driving technology. This has the potential to improve road safety, traffic management, and environmental impact by lowering both.

Availability, Number Four: Self-driving cars may make mobility easier for the elderly, people who cannot drive, and people with impairments. They provide for more freedom of movement and autonomy.

The potential impact of Waymo's efforts extends beyond increased road safety, reduced traffic congestion, more convenient transportation, and substantial breakthroughs in the logistics and delivery industries. These developments may lessen transportation's negative effect on the environment and have far-reaching consequences for urban planning.

In conclusion, cutting-edge research in AI and autonomous vehicles is being conducted at places like DeepMind and Waymo. Significant and potentially game-changing advances may result from their application to healthcare, transportation, logistics, and the creation of ethical artificial intelligence. As these initiatives develop and mature, they may lead to considerable improvements in many areas of society and economic growth.

9.3 Google's dedication to innovation is crucial to the company's history and its success. The company's culture, history, and strategic goal all show a dedication to pushing the frontiers of what's possible and producing revolutionary solutions that can revolutionize the way people live, work, and connect with the world.

In the early days of Google, Larry Page and Sergey Brin had a vision to foster a culture of invention. It was their goal to "organize the world's information and make it universally accessible and useful." Google's dedication to creating novel approaches to fixing tough issues was fueled by this goal statement.

X (previously Google X) moonshot projects are an example of Google's dedication to innovation and the company's desire to push the boundaries of technology. From autonomous vehicles and universal internet access to medical breakthroughs and environmentally friendly power sources, these initiatives aim to address some of the world's most pressing problems.

Thirdly, Research and Development - Google has a strong R&D division that focuses on investigating new technologies. Progress in areas such as AI, quantum computing, and machine learning are all examples. The corporation places a strong emphasis on funding research projects as a means of fostering innovation.

4. Open Source Contributions: - Google makes many of its technologies available to the open-source community and is a major contributor to open-source projects. This encourages teamwork and creativity beyond the company's doors, which has far-reaching consequences for tech advancement on a worldwide scale.

5. Investment in Startups and Acquisitions: - Google invests in startups and acquires firms that indicate potential for creative solutions. With this plan, the organization may more easily adopt cutting-edge tools and hire top-tier employees who share its values.

The Sixth Principle of User-Centric Innovation: - Users are at the heart of everything Google does. Whether it's through enhanced search algorithms, the introduction of new goods, or the fine-tuning of existing services, the company is always looking for new ways to improve user experiences and find solutions to real-world problems.

7. Ethical AI Development: - Google is heavily invested in the development of AI in a responsible and ethical manner. It has developed guidelines for AI study that stress justice, openness, and responsibility.

8. Environment and Long-Term Sustainability: - Google is committed to sustainable and ecologically acceptable actions. In an effort to reduce its impact on the environment, the corporation has committed to using only renewable energy. These actions show how serious it is about finding new ways to ensure a sustainable future.

9 Research and Development Laboratories for New Ideas: - Google has a global network of research labs, engineering offices, and innovation hubs. Collaboration, research, and the creation of new technology are all encouraged in such settings.

10] Dedication to Education and Training: - In order to foster the next generation of pioneers, Google funds a variety of educational and training initiatives. There are many opportunities to learn new skills and make new contributions to the technological world thanks to initiatives like Google for Education, Google AI, and online courses.

Google's dedication to innovation is not limited to its main industries of search and advertising. It includes a wide variety of efforts to improve society through technological innovation and to address some of the world's most serious problems. Google's dedication to innovation has not only defined the company's success but also had far-reaching effects on the whole technology industry. The company's continued exploration of the limits of possibility has resulted in groundbreaking discoveries that could one day help solve some of the world's most intractable problems.

Chapter 10
Google's Global Impact

10.1 Google is now one of the world's most powerful and pervasive digital companies thanks to the incredible global reach of its goods and services. The wide range of products offered by the firm covers many different markets and is made with a global clientele in mind. Here, we investigate the far-reaching effects of Google's offerings around the world:

As the most popular search engine in the world, Google Search ranks first. It serves practically every country in the world and is translated into more than 150 languages. Every day, billions of people use Google Search to explore the internet and learn new things.

Second, Google Chrome, which has a market share of more than 60% and is one of the most popular browsers in use today. Millions of people all around the world use it to connect to the internet, and it's available on a wide variety of platforms.

Thirdly, the Android operating system (OS) - created by Google - is the most widely used mobile OS worldwide. Most mobile devices run on it, including smartphones and tablets. Because of this widespread coverage, Google is able to offer its services and goods to mobile users all around the world.

4. Google Maps: - Google Maps is an essential navigation and mapping service utilized by people across the globe. It gives users information about nearby establishments and attractions as well as current traffic conditions. The reach of the service is global in scope.

Google Drive, Number Five: - Google Drive is a cloud-based storage and collaboration platform utilized by people of all walks of life and organizations of all sizes. Users can upload files to the cloud, share them with others, and work together on them.

YouTube is a Google-owned video-sharing website that is popular around the world. It's available in over 100 countries and provides material in numerous languages. Users from all across the world upload their own films to YouTube, giving the site a truly global reach.

7. Gmail - This is probably the most well-known email service in the world. It's a worldwide communication tool because it has users from all over the world and all walks of life.

Google Translate, number eight on this list, may help people all around the world communicate with one another by providing instant translations from and to hundreds of different languages.

9 Google Ads: - Google Ads offers advertising solutions for companies of all sizes, enabling them to access a worldwide audience with digital marketing campaigns.

Google Workspace (formerly known as G package) is a package of cloud-based productivity tools utilized by companies and organizations all over the world. Google Docs, Sheets, and Meet are all part of it, and they make it possible for people all over the world to work together and get more done.

Google Assistant (#11) is a voice-activated AI assistant that supports several languages and allows users to control their devices just by speaking to them.

12. Google Classroom: - Google Classroom is a widely used platform for online education and e-learning, linking teachers and students globally, especially during the COVID-19 pandemic.

Google's efforts to make its products and services available, inclusive, and adaptable to other languages, cultures, and locations have contributed to the company's global reach. The company's dedication to its customers has allowed it to become an integral part of people's lives all across the globe. The global availability and dependability of Google's services have been further bolstered by the company's investments in international data centers and infrastructure.

The more Google develops and diversifies its products and services, the more of an international impact they will have on people's ability to communicate, collaborate, and find their way around the Internet.

10.2 One of the most powerful corporations of the information age, Google has helped shape the internet and information access around the world. Its effects can be seen in a variety of contexts, from search algorithms to the evolution of the internet itself. Here, we talk about how Google has impacted the world wide web and how people gain access to information.

First, Dominance in Search Engines: - How individuals look for information online has been drastically altered by Google's search engine. Search innovations like PageRank have helped it deliver accurate and relevant results to users. Google Search soon became the world's most popular search engine and the go-to source for information.

Google's stated goal to "organize the world's information and make it universally accessible and useful" demonstrates the company's dedication to making information available to all people, regardless of their location or ability to understand English. The dissemination of information has been greatly facilitated as a result.

Thirdly, we offer support for multiple languages, ensuring that people from all walks of life can use Google to find what they need, in the language of their choice. Having content available in more than one language has increased its reach.

4. Open Source Initiatives: - Google is heavily involved in the open source community and has released several of its technologies under an open source license. Because of this dedication to open source, many useful tools and frameworks have been created that have influenced the design and usability of the internet.

5. The Mobile Revolution: - Thanks to Google's Android operating system, which is used by the vast majority of smartphones throughout the world, millions of people who had previously had little to no access to the internet now have it at their fingertips. Because of this, more people in impoverished regions can now gain access to the internet.

Online collaboration and communication have been revolutionized by Google's suite of internet services, which includes Gmail, Google Drive, and Google Docs. These services make available, anywhere in the world, the fundamental means of production and communication.

In addition to reshaping the internet advertising market, Google's advertising platform has helped innumerable websites and businesses commercialize their content and services, which in turn helps to maintain the digital ecosystem.

8. Mapping and Navigation: - The widespread adoption of Google Maps has drastically altered the ways in which the general public uses mapping and navigation services. The global mapping data it collects includes a plethora of information about locations, attractions, and more.

9. Promoting Web-Based Uniformity - Internet best practices and online standards have been aggressively advocated by Google. It was instrumental in the creation of HTML5, and it has pushed for the widespread use of HTTPS, which makes the web more secure.

Connectivity projects, such as Google's Project Loon, attempted to bring internet access to unserved and rural areas by deploying high-altitude balloons. While Project Loon has changed, the company's dedication to boosting connectivity remains obvious.

AI and ML, at Number Eleven - Voice assistants, smart search, and content recommendations are just a few examples of how Google's investments in AI and ML have revolutionized how people find and use information. These innovations improve users' ability to access and engage with digital content.

Google has played a pivotal, ever-evolving role in developing the internet and how people gain access to information online. The company has improved people's access to information all around the world through the creation of cutting-edge technology, support of open-source endeavors, and promotion of an accessible and open internet. Beyond only search, Google has had an impact on many other facets of online life, including social networking, travel, and entertainment, all of which contribute to the democratization of information and knowledge around the world.

10.3 Because of its revolutionary impact on culture, technology, and information access, Google will leave behind a lasting legacy. Since its start, Google has profoundly influenced the development of the Internet and the globe at large. In this piece, we consider Google's lasting impact on culture:

Google's primary goal is "to organize the world's information and make it universally accessible and useful," which has had a profound effect on how people gain access to information. The search engine's algorithms, such as PageRank, have revolutionized how we study, explore, and communicate by giving us access to a large trove of information in an instant.

2. Internet Ecosystem: Google's many services, such as Gmail and Google Drive, have become fundamental to the way we interact online and have a profound impact on our methods of communication, teamwork, and data storage. This has reshaped the ways in which we do business, learn, and socialize.

Google's Android and Chrome products have been instrumental in expanding internet access around the world. Millions of individuals all over the world can now take advantage of the information and opportunities available online.

Internet Marketing, Number Four: In addition to revolutionizing the digital advertising market, Google's advertising platform has helped innumerable companies and content producers generate revenue from their online activities. As a result of this economic impact, creativity and risk-taking have flourished.

5. Cartography and Direction-Finding: Google Maps has revolutionized the way we travel and discover new places. It's changed the way we travel and engage with the world around us by providing instant access to information from anywhere in the world.

Machine learning and AI are discussed in the sixth paragraph. The innovations in AI and ML that Google has introduced have completely changed the way we use computers. The use of voice assistants, search engines, and personalized suggestions have all grown commonplace because of how much they improve people's lives.

7.Contributions to Open Source Projects: Google's dedication to open-source projects has encouraged greater cooperation and new developments in the IT sector as a whole. It has led to the development of several tools, frameworks, and standards that help society as a whole.

8. Ecological Obligation: Google's sustainability ambitions include eliminating the company's carbon impact entirely. By taking this step, the corporation is demonstrating its commitment to promoting environmentally responsible and ethical business practices.

Learning New Skills and Expanding Your Knowledge Base In order to provide people with the necessary knowledge and abilities in the digital age, Google has invested in educational programs like Google for Education and Google AI. The educational system as a whole has been affected by this.

Constructing Morally Sound AI, Tenth Place: Google's efforts to promote the responsible growth of AI have helped establish best practices for the field. As a result of this effect, the tech sector is more open, equitable, and responsible.

 Self-driving cars, Waymo, and Verily are just a few of Google's moonshot projects with the potential to shake things up and change the world. Google's dedication to innovation is on full display in these new projects.

We will remember Google for the way it spread knowledge to the masses, brought people together, encouraged creativity and innovation, and advocated for the ethical creation of new technologies. Technology, accessibility, and communication all continue to be shaped by it, therefore it's clear that it has a lasting impact on society.

Google's legacy will continue to develop as the company grows and takes on new challenges. It will be shaped by the ethical standards it upholds, the environmental sustainability it promotes, and the global connectivity it fosters. We should expect Google to have a lasting impact on how we obtain information, how we get around online, and how we use technology in the future.

Milton Keynes UK
Ingram Content Group UK Ltd.
UKHW020252221123
432980UK00017B/1232

9 798868 985966